SEASONS OF FRIENDSHIP

By Marjolein Bastin

"Journey through the following pages with me as my brushes and paints bring to life some of my favorite memories of friendship, family and, of course, nature."

Marjolein, Aged 9

Mary Ann, Aged 6

Roberta, Aged 10

Margaret, Aged 9

WRITTEN AND ILLUSTRATED BY
Marjolein Bastin

EDITED BY
Margaret Tao

STYLED BY
Mary Ann Odom

DESIGNED BY
Roberta Abramson

A letter from Marjolein...

As I begin writing this, I look out of the window of my studio and spot my friend the robin. He is not a rare bird, but a good friend doesn't have to be a rare one. The European robin is one of my best outdoor companions. He keeps me company when I am working in the very early mornings—each workday begins at 6 a.m. It is very quiet then, with my family still deep asleep, and I am able to work very intensively in those lonely hours. When daylight comes— no, even earlier—when it is still pitch dark, the robin says hello to me with its wonderful, clear song. I imagine—total silence...darkness...and suddenly there is that song, clear as a star glittering in the night. All the other birds arrive later, when there is a little more light, and most of them just sing during their breeding season to defend their territory, to attract that beautiful, young feathered lady. The robin, however, is one of the few birds that sings the whole year round, so every day starts with my friend the robin.

I don't even need to look at the outside thermometer to know how cold it is. Just look at the birds. The robin has his winter coat on. He turns up the heat by fluffing up his feathers so that the warmth from his body stays within the down. The rounder he looks, the colder it is, and when he kneels down to cover his feet, better stay inside!!! It's too bad that we humans have no down or fur, but we manage. We sleep under down comforters… the down of our nature friends.

This is how the robin looks in the summer.

The same robin when it's cold: feathers out. Looks fatter, but isn't.

Now it's even so cold that he's warming his legs. He hangs his down coat over them.

Friendships between human beings are different in many ways from "friendships" between things in nature, but still there are some striking similarities. Both types of friendship are about giving and taking and needing one another to be complete. Just as we depend on our human friends for companionship and understanding, so the nature creatures depend on each other for many of their needs.

What would plants or flowers be without their friends the butterflies? There would be no pollination. The flowers know that when their friends come to call, they must offer them something that they particularly like— so they offer them pollen and nectar. When the guests arrive, they enjoy themselves with a wonderful meal!

The swallowtail butterfly is a wonderful example of how nature creatures depend upon one another. These butterflies need plants to shelter their eggs, nectar from flowers for nourishment, and Queen Anne's lace for their caterpillars to eat. When we began mowing the shoulders of the road very intensively in Holland, we were mowing away this butterfly's whole world. Soon we saw less and less of this beautiful butterfly because the nature friends it needed for its existence were gone. We do still mow, but much less and sometimes with a schedule that follows the needs of the butterflies. The Queen Anne's lace returned, and slowly the swallowtails are returning also.

Friendship means shelter. When it suddenly starts to rain after a warm summer day, or when the nights are growing colder, it is so good to have a place where you can hide and sleep. You often can find bumblebees under the thistles, dew still on their fur coats, sleepily awaiting the warm morning sunshine...

sort of like sleeping under the dining table.

A vase of spring, a bouquet made from the very first white flowers.

Gifts

Once I planted white grape hyacinths in the garden, which now fit well in this bunch of lilies of the valley, fritillaria, hound's-tongue, campanula, and the very last snowdrops.

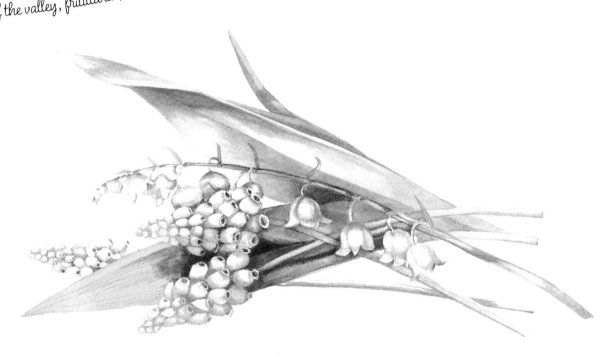

Gifts are such sweet expressions of friendship. When you truly care about someone else, you want to share with them a token of that caring. This token doesn't have to be expensive or rare to delight your friend — just heartfelt. It can be as simple as a bouquet of flowers, a feather, a shell, or anything that you know will bring joy, just because you cared enough to remember someone dear to you.

No, I didn't go far away on vacation, nor did I visit a shell museum. I received this magnificent collection of beach discoveries from a friend who lives in South Africa. After I placed everything on my worktable, I could see right away that this was too beautiful to be put immediately into my display case with my other treasures from far away. I have to let everyone see this first. Beautiful, isn't it?

"Now, I really feel like getting some nice mail," I said to Gaston recently when we drove through the gate after a day away. Then I found this exciting envelope lying in the mailbox! Feathers fluttered out, pieces of bark, leaves, and fruits – one even more exciting than the other...all the way from Australia.

Australia 35c

Australia $2

POSTPAK Packaging Products

POSTPAK Packaging Products

POSTPAK Packaging Products

WELLINGUP

20c

AUSTRALIA

95c

AUSTRALIA

COMMON WOMBAT

85c

AUSTRALIA
ANTARCTIC TERRITORY

Australia
MARRARA · VICTORIA

POSTPAK Packaging Products

$5

POSTPAK Packaging Products

Bastin (Libelle)

MA Haarlem

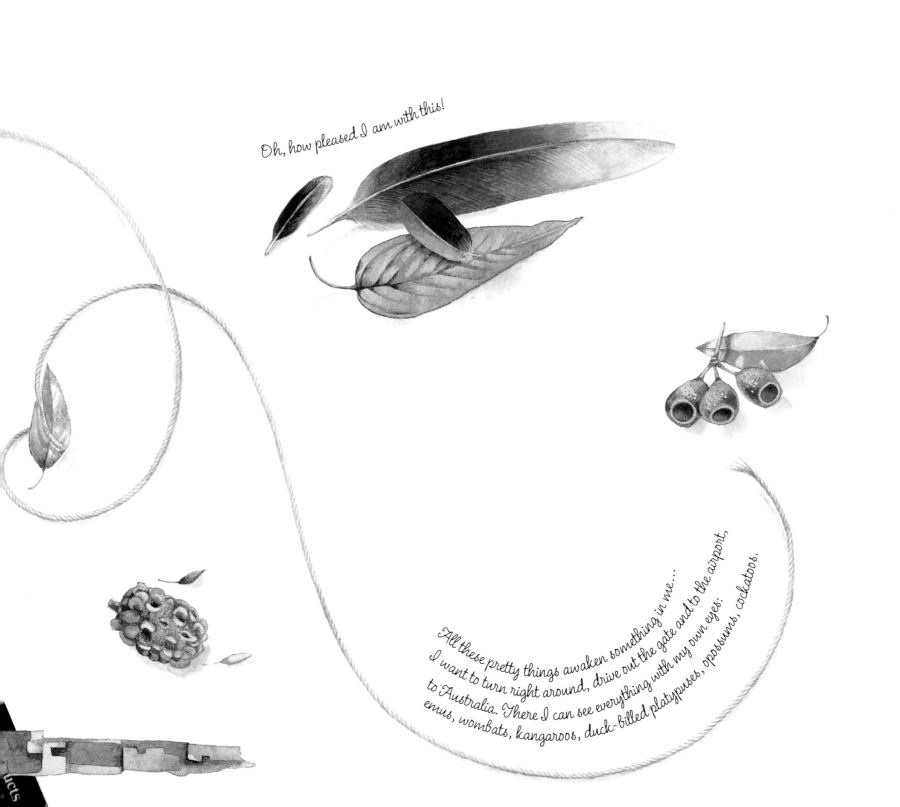

Oh, how pleased I am with this!

All these pretty things awaken something in me...
I want to turn right around, drive out the gate and to the airport,
to Australia. There I can see everything with my own eyes:
emus, wombats, kangaroos, duck-billed platypuses, opossums, cockatoos.

What a nice gift I received the other day! My neighbor had filled half a coconut with a mixture of suet and birdseed and put raffia around it. All I had to do was hang it up. What a happy surprise!

I saw so many splendid exotic birds in the zoo, one more colorful than the other. Actually, though, if you try to look at him "anew," our blue tit is just as exotic! What a shade of blue!! And that in combination with his vanilla-pudding-yellow belly…

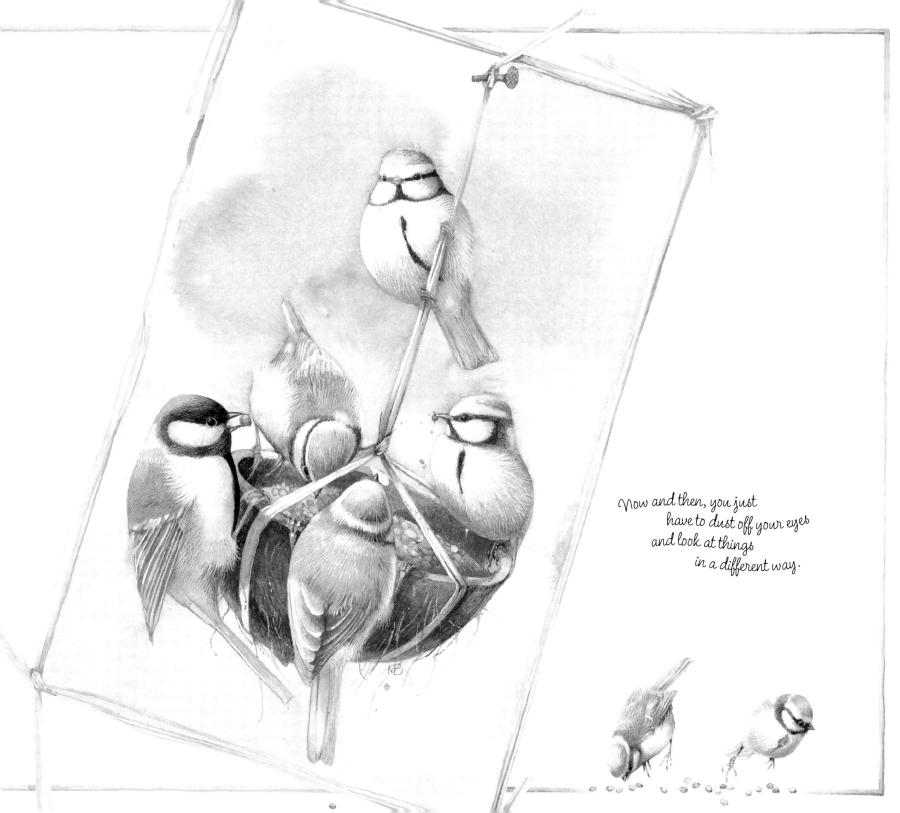

Now and then, you just
have to dust off your eyes
and look at things
in a different way.

Color

Just as we give gifts to our friends, nature also offers us priceless gifts if we only take the time to notice and receive them.

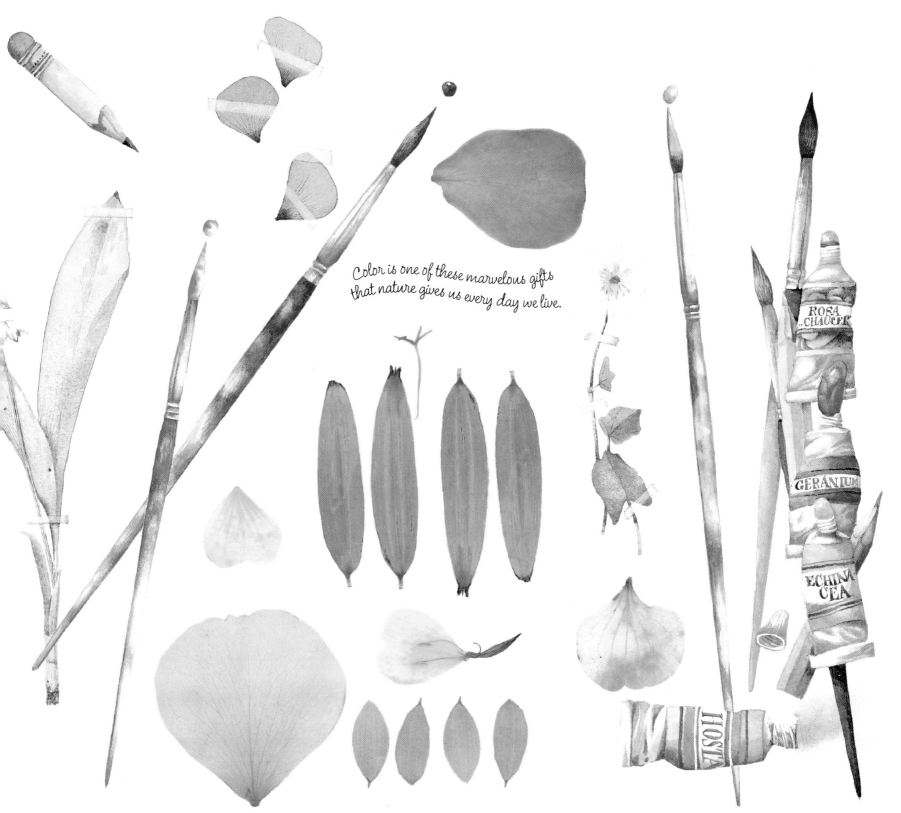

Color is one of these marvelous gifts
that nature gives us every day we live.

Green

Think about the first green leaves in early spring. It is as if nothing or no one has ever touched that color before. There are so many varieties of green...mosses, grass, leaves, and faraway greens that are created when you look over the hills and see the color fading from dark green to the lightest touch of pale bluish green, hardly green anymore, as if you did a watercolor drawing and almost forgot to use your paint tube...

Yellow

Most of the time, we don't even notice that everything around us has color. But sometimes we can't help but notice. Take, for instance, that field full of yellow prairie flowers. The beauty of it takes your breath away, so that you don't only see yellow, but you even feel it deep down. Now for the rest of your life, you will know— yellow is that field of flowers, and no other yellow you see after that will ever be as intense as that first experience with yellow.

Blue. Is there very much blue in nature? At first, I wasn't really sure, but then I noticed a small bunch of hydrangea flowers in front of me on my worktable. Then I started thinking about blue. Blue is the most beautiful, intense color—the blue of summer skies, blue skies—as if there is not a single problem in the whole world. Oh, the biggest "blue experience" I ever had was in Colorado when I saw a mountain bluebird for the first time in my life! I couldn't believe my eyes—this blue, this heavenly blue. I thought, when I make a painting of this bird, nobody in Holland will believe that this is real.

Blue

You can never hide blue in nature. Seeing those small blue butterflies dancing in the sky is like seeing small blue paint spots dancing as if they were still wet from my paintbrush. The most tender blue I know is the blue of the bird eggs carefully covered by the warm breast of their mother or father. Nothing is more hidden, more loved, and more beautiful. They are treasures that tell us the story of life and how life and love belong together.

Brown

When you think of brown, it creates no big excitement at first. Maybe it reminds you of late fall. But wait! Nature uses brown in a very special way—to give the young birds a good cover! Beautiful and colorful as their parents may be, the vulnerable young ones must hide in their brown coats until they are able to face the possible dangers in the big world outside. See these brown butterflies? When they dance above colorful flowers and catch the warm sunlight with their velvet wings, their color is not a dull color. Instead, it is a warm, enchanting range of beiges, browns, and golden colors. Finding a brown feather that a bird lost from his plumage is like finding a treasure. I never, ever leave one on the ground. Instead, I'll kneel down and take it as a gift from nature. You see, it is not only the bird itself that is beautiful and catches my attention, it is also that small detail, that one perfect feather, that is worth a closer look. Hold a feather in your hand—one brown feather— and you will realize that beauty uses color, but not necessarily bright color, to express itself.

Red

Red is poppies— the one red poppy in the green meadow or thousands of poppies blooming along the roadside in June. I remember driving with a friend through the hills in Tuscany on a warm June morning. We enjoyed views of endless hills, picturesque small towns, old castles…and poppies. Fields of poppies were scattered over the landscape. There is almost nothing more shocking to the eyes than the fire-red color of thousands of poppies. Now tone down that color a bit to the velvet, paler pink-red of raspberries. You see? Immediately you know what color I'm talking about. And when I think of that wonderful month of June, how could I ever forget about the color of the first cherries that appear just around my birthday…

This is the house where I grew up.

The teahouse by the river where I used to play.

Birthdays

Recently we were sitting near the river in Loenen aan de Vecht eating pancakes, and we suddenly saw three storks circling over our heads. I was delighted. Of course the storks would visit us here, I thought, because Loenen is the village where I was born! Years ago, they delivered me here! This incident brought to mind that old congratulatory telegram which my parents received two days after my birth in 1943. I also saved all of the other letters sent to my parents at my birth!! It's funny to read them.

Gelukwensch-Telegram

VEEL GELUK

Telegram uit *Loenen /. Vecht* den *18 Juni* 1943

Hartelijk Gefeliciteerd

met de Geboorte
van Uw Dochter

Afzender
Sopie Gorsselink.

Happy me!

Can you see the happiness on my face which resulted from being born into a world of love and care? Is there a better place to be than in the arms of your mother? What a richness!

My grandmother from Amsterdam sent me this card for my first birthday.

EEN jaar
is onze kleine puk,
Wij wenschen je
nog veel geluk.

ome

Please, please, please let me out into the exciting world named "Garden"!

Life is a feast!

My mother came home from the hospital with my baby sister, Babette! A bit later, Babette ended up in my old playpen.

A time of endless discovery — turning around each leaf, each stone; digging holes in the ground with one small finger; following busy bees and butterflies; trying to taste first raspberries, strawberries… and marbles.

Lucky me! Now I have freedom!

MB

I still remember my teenage birthdays so well... Every June for my birthday, my mother and sister rode their bikes to a field of rye, picked lots of poppies, cornflowers, and daisies— and decorated my chair with them.

I would so much like to have those cornflowers for my birthday again.

My son Mischa's tenth birthday was quickly approaching
while I was having one of the busiest times of my life with
the work I do for a magazine. I absolutely had to meet
the deadline for my weekly page about nature and also
think of something I could do that would
be really special for his tenth birthday.
Then I had an idea. I would make that
page in the magazine especially for him
so everyone in Holland would know
how important it is to be ten years old.
Since Mischa's favorite color was
Ferrari red, I decided to "help"
nature a little bit.

I made a red bumblebee, colored a yellow butterfly red (sorry, butterfly),
painted some red berries, and gave him a red fork for his breakfast.
Finally, I made a beautiful circle of red around his plate.
Now if only they made red wisteria...

Family

Family plays such a large part in some of our dearest memories, because our families — parents, sisters, brothers, grandparents, aunts, uncles — are really the very first friends we make in life.

When my father saw my mother for the first time, it was love at first sight! They shared so many things. Both of them were very romantic, and they both loved beauty and literature. Perhaps they were not rich in money — my father was a teacher, and my mother was just my mother — but they were so rich in feelings!! They lived in a most wonderful tiny town on a river. The garden was at the edge of the river and was full of flowers, fruits, birds, hens, and rabbits. The whole rich world surrounded them. How lucky I was to grow up in their safe and happy warmth.

Nearly fifty years later, I went back to that garden of happiness. Strangers live there now who don't know about the great joy that garden gave me so long ago. As I wandered around, so many forgotten memories flooded back to me. Suddenly I spotted an old watering can in a corner under an old pear tree. I thought I recognized it, but of course that was impossible after nearly fifty years—or was it? I asked the current owner, and he told me that the watering can was there when he bought the house many years ago. Slowly I walked to it and took it very carefully in my hand. So this was the old watering can from my childhood. I was so very happy that besides all the memories, there was this one other thing left from the paradise garden where I grew up so happily with two people who loved each other so dearly.

Our house is at the top of this old postcard.

Brug te Loenen a.d. Vecht

MOMMIE ♥

My mother—born in 1915 in Munich, Germany—with her parents.

While I was growing up, I thought my mother was just my mother. She took care of everything, helped, taught, and comforted. I loved her endlessly and needed her in the same amount. My mother and I were together from the moment I opened my eyes in the morning until the moment I kneeled down and said my prayers in the evening. I miss the long walks we took along the river, with the big trees bending over the luscious green grasses, reeds, and flowers. Now when I look back over those happy days, I see the time we shared in a different light. I realize that those times together with my mother not only brought me joy but also greatly influenced the path I walk along in my life today.

Voor Mammie

When I was about ten years old, I drew my mother March violets for Mother's Day. I wanted to share with her those velvet beauties with the incomparable scent that grew under our hedge. At that moment, they were the most beautiful things I could think of in the whole world. A diamond or something gold looked poor and pale in comparison to the tender, deep purple treasures I drew for her. I bought a frame out of my allowance so that the picture was "just like real." She hung it above their bed, in the middle between the two pillows.

POPPIE

My father was born in 1911 in Zwolle, the Netherlands.

My Father and I

I loved my father; I adored him, even though he was seldom there.
He was a teacher and a storyteller, and he did exciting things with me.
He gave me cookies, without realizing that my mother had forbidden them...
And that pipe smoke coming out of his nose! He would blow ringlets for me
in the air. Everybody in our small town knew him
and respected him. I felt proud to walk next
to him with my small hand
in his big hand.

At first glance, they are all the same tricolored violas. If you look a bit more closely, however, you see that they're all different.

Yet, they're all offspring of one viola that I planted in the garden last year. Our two children also have the same parent plant— and how different they are. They're growing just as fast as those violas. In a month, Mischa— after Sanna— is also leaving home. Twenty years together… Such a short time ago, they were still lying in that cozy little wicker crib. They've turned into nice violas. Different from the parent violas, but still a little bit the same.

Aged 4 and 5

Mischa and Sanna, dressed up for a special day at school.
Aged 6 and 7

In Switzerland, where we always spent the holidays. Aged 18 and 17

Our closeness with family creates a special bond, and in the same way, our ties with old friends can give us love, can give us a feeling of being "at home" and safe in our hearts. Sometimes no one knows you like an old friend, because you've shared with them the things that bring you joy— your dreams, your fears, your history. For this reason, an old friend is truly a treasure.

Old Friends

One of my oldest friendships is with nature. Just like a squirrel, I hide all my treasures from nature, because you never know. And just like the squirrel, I forget where. Sometimes I run across these treasures by accident, and it is like running into old, dear friends.

I was looking for the ink bottle and found this pretty, sea-green box again. It had once had a birthday present in it from New York. It will be handy, I thought, for storing my newest collection of feathers, and I opened the lid.

Too bad! I had forgotten it was already occupied by all kinds of discoveries from the windowsill (except the may bug and the jay feather). Wouldn't it be a shame to let something so beautiful disappear into the vacuum cleaner?

ASSICURATA CONVENZIONALE

750 ITALIA

Fetching the mail from the mailbox is always exciting. Will there be something nice in it? Not long ago, there was a sweet letter from Italy with a little box, crushed flat, full of little nature treasures. It was so pretty that I had to draw it right away. Thank you, Elisabetta!

There was another small package, all the way from South Africa, from a friend who once sent me two splendid bird nests. In a medicine box, packed in cotton, was this impressive rhinoceros beetle. She had found him in her garden.

RSA
BY AIRMAIL
PER LUGPOS
PAR AVION

MYSTECLIN

TAKE ONE
COMPLETE
NW MNR

MOREL
MEDICINE
H.B.VENTE

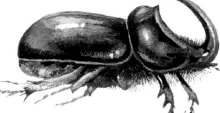

Rhinoceros Beetle

RSA R1

Trichocaulon cactiforme   Hein Botha 1988

My friend Susan lives in Kansas City in the middle of America. An American robin built a nest in her arbor. Susan followed everything carefully, since the nest was right by her window. Sure enough, one morning the first egg lay there, so flawless and sea-green in color. There the story stops for the robin: an overenthusiastic dog chased her away, and she didn't dare come back. How sad.

And yet that's not the end of the story. The nest just sat there, with that one beautiful egg in it, as though everything had been for naught. Susan sent it to me…by mail…terribly well-packed. That beautiful blue egg in the nest made a journey of thousands of miles in a big, fat Boeing jet. I was so moved when I opened the package here at my worktable and saw that flawless, sea-green egg lying in the dark nest. It's now one of my most delicate "possessions." If a bird had hatched from it, it would never have been able to fly that far.

Paris 1965

Gaston and I met at the Academy
of Arts in 1960, were friends in '61,
engaged in '64, and married
in '67. Gaston's mother
took this picture of us on one
of our many trips to Paris.

This is the house where his family lived before World War II. Of course,
our honeymoon was to Paris again, but this time (for the first time) without his mother!!!

Thirty years later, we're still the biggest friends. We share everything, and it works! I love him as I did then. I hope he feels the same. Think so.

How can I begin to describe my marriage and deep friendship with Gaston? How better than with the images of nature that immediately come to my mind when I think of our relationship. Quite simply, Gaston is the hedge around my garden. He keeps out the harsh wind and provides shade and shelter so that I have a quiet place where I can nurture my flowers and create exciting and beautiful things…things I couldn't do without that dear hedge. We each have our own important roles, just like two birds building a nest. One bird makes a strong foundation with sturdy branches, and the other bird decorates the nest with all kinds of feathers, wool, small straws. Both need each other to make the nest a home. I couldn't do without Gaston, and I think he couldn't do without me. He is my best friend.

Pets

Why is there such a strong friendship between humans and their pets?

When you measure this relationship in love, there isn't a distinction between you and your dog or your cat. They are simply part of you. You can communicate without words, exchange feelings, and I am sure they know you better than many people know you. I have many friends around me whom I love dearly, and they love me, but there is still a part of me which can only be filled by a dog. Just a dog.

I have always had animal friends. Before I could walk, I played with bugs and other very small creatures. Before I could talk, my mother took me out in the baby carriage. Suddenly my mother saw me laughing and turning deep red in my face: it was excitement, pure love!! I had just seen my first dog!! I couldn't talk, but I expressed my love very clearly.

My dearest dog friend is my sweet companion Saartje.
I am part of my dog, and my dog is part of me.
I know that her whole life through she will be with me.
She will love me, unconditionally, whatever I do.
Where I am, Saar is. Early in the morning, she
bumps down the stairs behind me. If I am
drawing, she lies under my table. Many times
she rests her head on my feet, so that I
don't dare to move until I get a cramp.
If I go for a walk, she goes along.
Always together—the best of friends.

I didn't see Saar growing old because she was around me all the time. Oh yes, she was a little stiff and, oh yes, from time to time she had her bad humors. She slept more and deeper and became deaf through the years, but we managed together. We didn't take those long walks anymore, and I talked to her in "body language." She was the dearest dog I've ever had, and because she was so dear to me, I had the feeling she would never leave me. When she died in my arms, when she laid her head in my hand for the last time, I lost a friend.

We buried her in my herb garden, because that is the place where I like to be when the world is too busy and I need a rest. Every time I come to pick some chives, it's just as though she's walking around me again, as though she can soon come out from behind the greenhouse. Bye, dear, dear friend. Thank you for everything you gave me without even knowing it.

On my way home, for the first time without Saar's company,
I picked a few branches of honeysuckle. Crying.
Walking through the orchard between the herb
garden and the house, I picked a few cherries,
and on the ground, I found the wing of a butterfly…
After I arranged everything on my table,
the honeysuckle, the cherries, and the empty collar,
I started to draw her last portrait. I thought
by doing it I could paint her back. I really
could feel her when I painted her! This time
it wasn't a watercolor painting;
it was made with my tears.

After some time passed, I began to realize
that even when the special ones in our lives
are no longer with us, we still feel
very close to them. Our bond with them is so
strong and our memories of them so vivid that it
is as if we can communicate with them still.
Friendship is so strong it survives everything.

And that's what the magazine did: quickly forwarded it. The next day, this envelope lay on my table. And when I opened it, this photograph fell out. Annelies with her dog Boris, who was then nine weeks old. My heart started beating faster: a Jack Russell, with spots on his head just like Saar had. Saar, whom I still missed terribly. Reading further, I couldn't believe my wet eyes. To make a long and lovely story short, the letter ended with, "If you want him, you may have him." When I dialed the telephone number, my knees were shaking. It couldn't be true... Thank you, Annelies! Welcome, Boris, Boris Bastin!

Now Boris is living with us. Where I am, Boris is. Soon Annelies will come to see how well Boris is doing here. Right, Boris? Woof!

a.u.b. snel doorsturen

Libelle redak
tav. Marjolein
Postbus 1
2000 MA Haarle

s.v.p. even
liet'

BORIS

Boris geboren 24-12-94

Boris is unrecognizable. Boris has been groomed, professionally and drastically, for two and a half hours.
When we came to pick him up, we saw a broom by an enormous pile of hair. Next to it stood a dog whom we didn't know...
until he began to bark and whine at us: Boris!!! How handsome he has become! He reminds me of a Renaissance painting.
If I had lived in the sixteenth century, my consort would have had a painter paint a sweet portrait of my cuddly little dog.

BORIS

24-12-94

• M·BASTIN •

Aren't new friends wonderful?!

Boris, as well as
being very sweet,
you're also very
handsome. Whatever,
thinks Boris.
I'm just cold.
Naked Boris.

In the year 1995, my consort, Gaston, takes a nice photograph of him.
The portrait I will paint myself.

I think new friends are so exciting because they give us the chance to experience new things, to learn, to grow, to share so much.

New Friends

We're going to America, which is full of all kinds of new friends and nature friends. While walking around the Midwestern prairie, it becomes clear to me that nature here in the heart of America is so different from home...different birds, different flowers, different sounds, different aromas.

I want to show that to everyone in Holland. I want to share this beauty, this richness, these new friends.

If I had to choose whether color,
shape, or aroma is more important,
I think I would choose aroma.

For me, aroma is even stronger than the message you receive from your eyes or ears,
because aroma can easily take you back in time to your childhood— or even further back.
Nothing can evoke an old memory more powerfully than a long-forgotten scent. I love to play
with dear memories by smelling different flowers and remembering... When I was a toddler, my mother
washed me with lilac soap, and when I was a bit older, the aroma of wisteria blooms
filled my bedroom on sultry spring evenings. Now, in America, I shove my nose
into a bouquet of sweet peas and I am immediately transported back to my
girlfriend's garden in Amersfoort in the fifties! Completely forgotten, but now back crystal-clear!

I hope that lilacs, wisteria, and sweet peas are blooming in Paradise. It almost can't be otherwise.

The most beautiful birds here in Colorado are the mountain bluebirds, which are such an unbelievably beautiful blue! We discovered a nest-building pair in an aspen tree. Can it be more beautiful, that heavenly blue on a cream-white tree trunk?

All the trees have black scars to about six feet high. That's because the deer eat the bark.

Under another aspen tree, we found a cleaned-out nest. Was a raccoon the culprit?
He likes eggs. In addition to stalks, the nest was made with feathers and hair.

This is a hair from a horse.

I draw the eggs back in again, performing magic with my brush.
Now all it needs is a bird to hatch them…

Exciting colored feathers from birds I don't know.

I think our Dutch jays look so exotic with those blue feathers on their wings, but you have jays here... A delight, no, a sensual delight, for my brush.

I can find him in the book I purchased to help me identify unfamiliar birds: scrub jay.

Then here's a bird sitting in a tree with all those pretty fruits. It looks like some kind of chestnut tree. I still have to buy a tree book.

A jay who lives in the bushes.

How quickly the time flies when you're enjoying it like this.
We have our last picnic on the flower-covered shoulder of the road
next to these mailboxes—together with American sparrows.

Good-bye, America! We must go home tomorrow. Right away I'm going to start drawing all the things I've seen here and enjoyed so much.

Here we are at home again, and I'm already remembering all the wonderful sights and sounds from our journey. Seeing a sparrow in our yard reminds me of our recent visit to New York. Central Park overwhelmed and excited me more than anything else in the city. All those birds in the heart of one of the biggest and busiest cities in the world! They were so different from our birds in Europe, one even more beautiful than the other. I immediately felt at home when I spotted an old friend, our Dutch house sparrow. He normally looks for a safe cavity such as a hole in a wall or in a thick, dense shrub to build his home, but this young man discovered a special place for his house. He and his girlfriend were still furnishing it like crazy, and I had a nice time observing them. More than a hundred years ago, the house sparrow was brought to New York by immigrants from Europe. Now these sparrows are widespread throughout the United States.

No soccer or football at anytime

The New York City Department of Parks and Recreation

Just as I discovered a little bit of Europe in America, I am now finding a little bit of America in my Dutch flower garden. I recognize in my perennial borders all kinds of flowers that were in full bloom in the prairie near Kansas City!

We saw the purple Liatris on the prairie, just like our Dutch Evening Primrose.

BLAZING STAR

EVENING PRIMROSE

PURPLE CONEFLOWER

We also saw purple Coneflowers growing on the prairie— and it blooms here in the garden, as well as Echinacea.

We also saw the Horsemint, which we call Monarda. The variety I have is Prairie Night. Now I understand.

HORSEMINT

DAYLILY Ah, I thought when I saw the daylily along the highway, another American! No sir, what did I read in my American flower book? "Originally from Europe. Brought by the first pioneers, now widespread throughout America." Funny to see the influence we have on each other. They have Europe on the shoulders of the road, and we have America in the garden!

MB

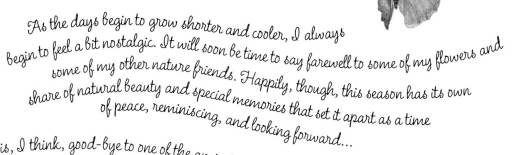

Memories

As the days begin to grow shorter and cooler, I always begin to feel a bit nostalgic. It will soon be time to say farewell to some of my flowers and some of my other nature friends. Happily, though, this season has its own share of natural beauty and special memories that set it apart as a time of peace, reminiscing, and looking forward...

This is, I think, good-bye to one of the ancient fruit trees in our orchard. Every year a pair of finches nested in its flowery crown. The main trunk is broken, and nice moss-covered twigs keep falling off. Far too many...

The fallen pears are stewing in the sun on the hay under the old trunk. A lot of them have begun to ferment, and they're attracting butterflies, wasps, flies, and even bumblebees. It's now deadly quiet — not a breath of wind. All you hear is the gnawing of the wasps, the dry rustling of the butterfly wings, and the humming of the bumblebees. The hay smells like earlier vacations.

What a splendid farewell reception. From the orchard to the kitchen with my box of pears, I am followed by a happy band of butterflies and wasps. Now the ants are running around my drawing table. They must have been in the pears, too. Good-bye, old pear tree, good friend... thank you.

All these seeds will carry through to next year.

Where now there are withered brown clumps, flowers will bloom again next year.

It is so difficult for me to say good-bye to my colorful summer flower garden. Week after week some of the color disappears. Here and there a faithful rose is still blooming...

The wild marjoram sowed thousands of new marjoram plants.

Still? Or already?

Protected under the walnut tree, a March violet dares to bloom.

Awakened by the warmth on my table, a ladybug crawls out of a rolled-up leaf.

Early in the morning, I wait until I hear my old friend the robin sing to open the curtains. Then it's still dark, but the morning light begins to glimmer at the edge of the woods. Today there's a surprise: it snowed a little, and everything is frosted white, magnificent and peaceful. As soon as the sun is up, everything will melt. It can only be held onto on paper.

When I see the first snow of winter,
I can't help but remember my very first snowman!
I remember so well waking up early,
too early, running to the window to open the curtains,
and holding my breath. The world had changed
overnight, and down there was a landscape
from my fairy-tale book!!!

After breakfast—never eaten as quickly as then—I made the first snowman in the new world. I remember rolling the big snowballs for the body of the snowman, starting with a small one, rolling on and on through the whole garden until it was so big I couldn't move it anymore. Hopefully, it was just in front of the window so that my mother could see what I had achieved. I remember how difficult it was to place the third ball, his head, on the top. It fell down many times. I knocked on the window with my wet mitten to ask my mother for a few pieces of black coal to make eyes and buttons on his belly. His nose was made of a big carrot. The crown of my snowman, a hat, was provided by my father. Wow, was I proud! When the work was finally done and my parents looked through the window at the result, I really felt like a snow queen. I had created something very beautiful that wasn't there one hour ago—just from that pure white snow!

Christmas is such a happy way to end the year! There are so many memories…

I can still see it so clearly before me: the glass Christmas tree bird from my childhood. I almost dare not draw it, because it wasn't unusual or expensive, but it was the most beautiful thing that we used to have on the Christmas tree. Every year, we were afraid that it would be broken when we opened the rickety box. Except for that, all we had were ordinary ornaments. We laid cotton on the branches so that it looked like it had snowed…

Christmases at home were simple and cozy. Lying under the tree, I tried to imagine what it was like there in that stable in Bethlehem. With my eyes shut tight, I saw the shepherds in the field, under the black velvet sky strewn with stars. On that night, the world changed… As my father read the Christmas story aloud, I no longer needed to hear the words. I already knew how the miracle went. In my thoughts, I was one of the shepherds, and I had brought a lamb.

Now there is much more hanging on our Christmas tree than back then. Instead of twenty shaky, dripping real candles in metal clip holders, there are a hundred electric lights on the tree—plugged in, and when we sing "Silent Night, Holy Night," my eyes get wet, because of the simplicity and the quiet, and also a bit because of remembering the way it used to be.

I hope I have given you a glimpse of the joy that the true treasures in life have given me— the rewards of friendship, the wonder of nature, that special bond with family. These are the things that bring beauty to my life— no, not the beauty of glittering things, jewels, or things you buy when you have a lot of money. It is the beauty of things you can find around you everywhere and always— when you take the time to see things as you did when you were a child. Maybe when you were younger, you had a treasure box in your bedroom? There could have been anything in it. I remember there were stones in mine— no rare ones, but just a strange black one with a white rim. There was a feather in the box, a dead bee I found on the windowsill, and the biggest acorn from the tree in our garden. Well, you can still have a treasure box, and you also can put abstract beauties in it, like the beams of the sun on a misty fall morning and the black velvet sky speckled with thousands of stars. Don't forget to include memories of dear friendships, cherished family members, favorite pets. One of the treasures I recently put in my treasure box was the wing of a butterfly. I saw it just before I nearly stepped on it. It was a little wonder there, lying on the cold and brown ground— it held a message of beauty. He has a home in my treasure box now, and I painted him for you to share something with you, to give you something. I think it is one of the most beautiful things I ever found.

I could go on forever; my treasure box is so full of little wonders. Please, never put a lid on your box. It has to be open forever. And if you close it and forget about it for a time, open it again. It is so simple, yet its joys can last a lifetime.

Love,

Marjolein Bastin

JANUARY

	1	2	3	4	5	6	7
1	2	3	4	5	6	7
8	9	10	11	12	13	14
15	16	17	18	19	20	21
22	23	24	25	26	27	28
29	30	31				

Special people, dates, events, memories, reflections to put in your "treasure box"...

FEBRUARY

1 2 3 4 5 6 7
8 9 10 11 12 13 14
15 16 17 18 19 20 21
22 23 24 25 26 27 28
29

MARCH

1	2	3	4	5	6	7
8	9	10	11	12	13	14
15	16	17	18	19	20	21
22	23	24	25	26	27	28
29	30	31				

APRIL

1 2 3 4 5 6 7
8 9 10 11 12 13 14
15 16 17 18 19 20 21
22 23 24 25 26 27 28
29 30

MAY

1	2	3	4	5	6	7
8	9	10	11	12	13	14
15	16	17	18	19	20	21
22	23	24	25	26	27	28
29	30	31				

JUNE

1 2 3 4 5 6 7
8 9 10 11 12 13 14
15 16 17 18 19 20 21
22 23 24 25 26 27 28
29 30

JULY

1 2 3 4 5 6 7
8 9 10 11 12 13 14
15 16 17 18 19 20 21
22 23 24 25 26 27 28
29 30 31

AUGUST

1	2	3	4	5	6	7
8	9	10	11	12	13	14
15	16	17	18	19	20	21
22	23	24	25	26	27	28
29	30	31				

SEPTEMBER

1 2 3 4 5 6 7
8 9 10 11 12 13 14
15 16 17 18 19 20 21
22 23 24 25 26 27 28
29 30

OCTOBER

1 2 3 4 5 6 7
8 9 10 11 12 13 14
15 16 17 18 19 20 21
22 23 24 25 26 27 28
29 30 31

NOVEMBER

1 2 3 4 5 6 7
8 9 10 11 12 13 14
15 16 17 18 19 20 21
22 23 24 25 26 27 28
29 30

DECEMBER

1 2 3 4 5 6 7
8 9 10 11 12 13 14
15 16 17 18 19 20 21
22 23 24 25 26 27 28
29 30 31

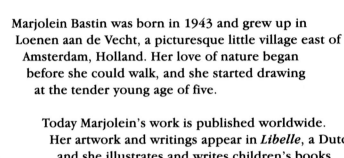

Marjolein Bastin was born in 1943 and grew up in
Loenen aan de Vecht, a picturesque little village east of
Amsterdam, Holland. Her love of nature began
before she could walk, and she started drawing
at the tender young age of five.

Today Marjolein's work is published worldwide.
Her artwork and writings appear in *Libelle*, a Dutch magazine,
and she illustrates and writes children's books
featuring the charming character Vera the Mouse.
Her unique work can also be found on greeting cards
and a variety of gift products.

Marjolein lives with her husband and manager,
Gaston, and their dog, Boris, near Arnhem,
Holland. She and Gaston have two grown children,
a son, Mischa, and a daughter, Sanna. The Bastins
place great value on their family and personal relationships.